What If Soldiers Fought with Pillows?

TRUE STORIES OF IMAGINATION AND COURAGE

For Alex and Juliana—sometimes a bad dream can have a happy ending —H.C.

For a peaceful world —S.B.

What If Soldiers Fought with Pillows?

TRUE STORIES OF IMAGINATION
AND COURAGE

Written by
Heather Camlot

Illustrated by
Serge Bloch

OWLKIDS BOOKS

We do not need magic to change the world. We carry all the power we need inside ourselves already: we have the power to imagine better.

—J.K. Rowling

Where does your imagination take you?

Maybe you see yourself traveling back in time, blasting off into space, or battling supervillains with your superstrength. But what if your imagination could also help you come up with solutions for real-world crises, such as war, famine, and human-rights violations? Sound impossible?

What if the impossible was actually possible?

When we ask big, fantastical questions, we may just discover new ways to change the world for the better. Our imagination can help shape the future by daring us to picture the world as we'd like it to be.

The people and organizations in the following stories had an idea about how they could make a difference. But more importantly, they decided to take that idea and turn it into action. In our imagination, we can do anything and be anyone. That can be true in reality too.

What if
soldiers fought with
pillows instead of
pistols **?**

During the Second World War, the US Army trained its men to kill or be killed. One soldier would do neither.

A deeply religious man, Desmond Doss was willing to serve in the war but refused to carry a weapon—he carried a Bible instead. And because of this, he was bullied by fellow soldiers. One officer even wanted him discharged for mental illness.

But Doss wouldn't change his mind. He wanted to save lives, not take them. He became a medic and was classified a conscientious objector because of his refusal to carry a weapon.

On May 5, 1945, in Okinawa, Japan, during one of the bloodiest battles of the Second World War, Doss's unit was ordered to capture the Maeda Escarpment, nicknamed Hacksaw Ridge, no matter the cost. But after the Americans had scaled the steep rock cliff to secure the ridge, the Japanese attacked. The Americans retreated quickly, leaving the wounded stranded.

Doss, however, stayed with those left behind.

He carried each injured soldier to the edge of the escarpment and lowered him to safety. It took twelve hours, yet somehow Doss didn't get hurt.

When he was injured weeks later, Doss treated his own wounds so another medic wouldn't have to risk his life getting to him. He was finally put on a stretcher hours later but rolled off to give it to a soldier in worse shape. While waiting for help, Doss was injured again. He made himself a splint and crawled to an aid station.

Doss never hurt or killed an enemy soldier. He did, however, save seventy-five of his own men that day on Hacksaw Ridge. And for his service, he became the first conscientious objector to receive the highest American military award, the Congressional Medal of Honor.

What if fighter pilots dropped seeds instead of bombs?

Everyone needs food to survive. But missiles, tanks, and AK-47s? Not so much.

Around the globe, 815 million people go hungry every day. And yet in 2017, the world increased its military spending to US$1.7 trillion. For the organization Food Not Bombs (FNB), it's incomprehensible that so much money goes to the military when so many struggle to afford food.

FNB was founded in 1980 after a young man named Brian Feigenbaum was arrested during a protest to stop construction of a nuclear power station. His friends tried to raise money for his legal fees … by holding bake sales. They didn't make much, but it did lead to an idea for a way to protest war, poverty, and environmental destruction.

Using surplus food from restaurants and stores, FNB began preparing vegetarian and vegan meals in parks and other public locations and sharing them with those in need. To this day, conversation is encouraged at these gatherings, especially around spending tax dollars on people, education, and healthcare, not guns and ammunition.

When Feigenbaum's friends began, they had little money and no political power. Today, there are hundreds of FNB chapters around the world. Some volunteers have been arrested, threatened, and even killed for their nonviolent activism to feed the hungry and starve the military budget. But that hasn't stopped FNB. It continues to feed those in need—from rescue workers after the 9/11 attacks in the US to protesters trying to end dictatorship in Tunisia—proving that food is a powerful tool for social change.

What if battlegrounds were soccer fields and spectators cheered for every team?

When a West African country was at war with itself, one legendary soccer player found a way to help his people unite rather than fight.

October 8, 2005, was a day that would go down in history for Ivory Coast: its national soccer team, nicknamed Les Éléphants, qualified for the World Cup for the first time.

But that wasn't the only significant event that day. As the players, who came from all across the country, sang and danced in the locker room, Didier Drogba, the team's star striker, was handed a microphone. Les Éléphants gathered before the TV cameras. "We proved today that all of the Ivory Coast can live together, can play together for the same objective: to qualify for the World Cup," said Drogba, a hero in Ivory Coast, where a brutal civil war between the rebel-held north and the government-held south had been waging for three years. "Today we beg you … please lay down all the weapons."

People listened. Both sides of the civil war declared a ceasefire and started peace talks. And in 2007, a peace agreement was signed.

But a unified country doesn't happen overnight, and so Drogba pitched a wild idea: hold one of the 2008 Africa Cup of Nations qualifying games in the northern town of Bouaké, a rebel stronghold.

The plan worked. When Ivory Coast beat Madagascar 5–0, fans from both sides of the civil war—regardless of ethnicity, religion, or hometown—united to cheer for their country.

"I have won many trophies in my time," the legendary soccer player told a reporter, "but nothing will ever top helping win the battle for peace in my country."

What if

Navy SEALs balanced balls on their noses or played horns?

US Navy SEALs take on some of the most dangerous missions in the military, but even their toughest training can't help them bring joy to children who have fled their homes and left everything they know behind.

"You know what we miss most? We miss laughter, to have fun, to enjoy ourselves," some young Bosnian refugees wrote to children in Barcelona, Spain, through a school solidarity project. The Bosnian children were living in the Veli Jože refugee camp in Croatia after having escaped the Bosnian War, which had forced their families to flee their country. The war would last nearly four years.

Their message gave the Spanish students an idea. A funny idea. They raised money to send a clown to the refugee children.

That clown, Tortell Poltrona, arrived in Croatia in February 1993. Once there, he made the kids smile. Then he made the kids laugh. And then he made a decision.

Soon after his visit, Poltrona founded the organization Clowns Without Borders. He had seen with his own eyes how laughter had helped make life a little better for the hundreds of young refugees and realized that he and other circus artists could help children all over the world. Today, the international organization sends circus and street performers, actors, magicians, musicians, and of course, clowns to entertain hundreds of thousands of children in crisis areas each year.

The work of Clowns Without Borders proves that while a big old belly laugh may not solve the world's problems, it can put those problems on hold. At least for a little while.

What if battle lines were drawn with paintbrushes and all the colors of the rainbow?

With one painting, Spanish artist Pablo Picasso proved that art can change the way we see, think, and act.

In 1937, Spain was in a civil war. General Francisco Franco's Nationalists wanted to overthrow the Republican government and asked the governments of Nazi Germany and Fascist Italy for help.

On April 26, German and Italian warplanes flew over Guernica, a Basque town that sided with the Republicans. One hundred thousand pounds of explosives and incendiary bombs were dropped over three destructive hours.

The town burned for three days. Seventy percent of the buildings were destroyed. But more than that, the air attack deliberately targeted and killed innocent civilians.

Pablo Picasso was living in France at the time. After learning about the massacre in his homeland, he poured his rage into his work. The result was the massive painting *Guernica*. Picasso filled *Guernica* with horrific images—a mother holding her dead child, a fallen soldier, a house engulfed in flames— that illustrate the realities of war: death, destruction, human suffering.

Guernica was created for the Spanish pavilion during the 1937 Paris exposition. The painting was then sent around the world, to bring attention to the atrocities of the Spanish Civil War and to raise money for refugees. Today, *Guernica* hangs in the Reina Sofía Museum in Madrid, Spain.

One of the most powerful anti-war paintings ever, *Guernica* has become a universal symbol of the horrors and inhumanity of war. It has been reimagined by artists, used during protests, and has inspired an international children's art project for peace.

What if
everybody showed up to a
political party with their
dancing shoes on**?**

In the fight for peace and survival, ballet beats bullets for one Palestinian dancer.

When the Islamic State took control of parts of Syria and Iraq, it enforced a strict interpretation of Islamic law and forbade many things, including dancing. Ahmad Joudeh, a Palestinian born and raised in a refugee camp in Syria, had "Dance or Die" tattooed in Sanskrit on the back of his neck. If Islamic State militants ever made good on their threats to behead him for dancing, he wanted these to act as his final words.

Joudeh had secretly taught himself to dance after seeing a ballet at age eight. When he was sixteen, he was accepted to the Enana Dance Theater, Syria's main ballet company. Five years later, in 2011, the Syrian Civil War broke out. The following year, Joudeh's home was destroyed during an attack on the refugee camp.

Still, he kept dancing. He taught dance to children, including some orphaned by the war, and studied at the Higher Institute of Dramatic Arts, situated in a part of the Syrian capital of Damascus that the Islamic State did not control. Then, in the summer of 2016, a Dutch TV journalist made a documentary about Joudeh and his incredible determination to keep dancing despite war and militant threats.

The director of the Dutch National Ballet saw the documentary, raised money, and brought Joudeh to the Netherlands to study dance—just before he would have to serve in the Syrian army and give up his dream.

Now a professional dancer and choreographer, Joudeh does everything he can to help others—from sharing his story, to raising money for refugees, to dancing in special performances that bring awareness to victims of war and promote peace around the world.

What if the rules of war were the same as the rules at school?

Even in war, there are rules to follow—rules meant to ensure soldiers act honorably. One Second World War pilot took them to heart.

On December 20, 1943, American second lieutenant Charlie Brown and his crew were on their first mission together, bombing an aircraft plant in Bremen, Germany. During the mission, Brown's plane was hit badly.

From the ground, German second lieutenant and ace pilot Franz Stigler spotted Brown's plane flying low. Stigler knew that if he downed the bomber, he'd be eligible for the prestigious Knight's Cross award.

Once in pursuit, though, Stigler saw that the bomber's tail gunner—the crewman at the back—was dead. Curious, he pulled alongside the plane and, seeing the terrible shape it was in, was amazed it could still fly. He tried signaling to Brown and the co-pilot to surrender over Germany—at least as prisoners of war, they'd have a chance to survive. Wide-eyed with disbelief, they shook their heads. So Stigler flew alongside the crippled bomber, hoping his countrymen below would see his plane and not fire. When both planes safely reached the North Sea, Stigler saluted goodbye.

In Nazi Germany, if you didn't shoot down the enemy, you could be punished by being shot yourself. Stigler knew this and still chose not to follow orders. He couldn't fire on a defenseless plane and crew. It would be dishonorable. It would be the action of a monster.

Brown couldn't forget that day. Decades later he looked for Stigler—and found him living in Canada. Almost forty-seven years after meeting in the air over Germany, they met face to face in Seattle, Washington. Together they embarked on a new mission: to share their incredible story with young and old—from students to veterans—across North America, not as feared enemies but as close friends.

What if
innocent civilians
could be airlifted
by music?

Music has the power to move your body and boost your mood. And as a group of young Senegalese proved, it also has the power to inspire a generation to vote.

In 2011, crowds gathered across Senegal to watch some of the biggest hip-hop artists in the country perform. But these were no ordinary concerts. They were a stage for change.

The performers were members of Y'en a Marre, a youth movement founded by hip-hop artists and journalists. Y'en a Marre is French for "we're fed up" or "enough is enough." The group was tired of the corruption and poverty under the West African country's president, Abdoulaye Wade, who had decided to run for a controversial third term.

Hip-hop in Senegal has long discussed politics. "Our responsibility is to look at the situation in the country and do something about it, say something about it," Thiat, a rapper and founding member of Y'en a Marre, told MTV.

As the 2012 presidential election got closer, their music demanded action—lyrics told Wade he was no longer wanted and explained how a voter card is power. And with 65 percent of Senegalese under thirty, Y'en a Marre had many listening.

But members didn't just sing their message. They went door to door to register more than three hundred thousand young voters and encourage everyone to go to the polls. They spoke about the need for a New Type of Senegalese (or NTS): citizens who were engaged and aware, and could move the country forward through informed and nonviolent action.

The election was one of peaceful Senegal's most tumultuous: clashes between police and protestors left at least six dead, and some Y'en a Marre rappers were targeted by snipers.

But Y'en a Marre wouldn't be silenced. Its activism contributed to Wade's losing the election, proving that hip-hop can be a poetic political force for democracy.

What if a theater of war had costumes and musical numbers?

Cambodia has such a long circus tradition, you can find carvings of acrobats, jugglers, clowns, magicians, and contortionists on ancient temple ruins. This artistic past helped modern Cambodians heal after decades of war.

When communist leader Pol Pot's brutal Khmer Rouge regime took power after a five-year civil war in 1975, the arts were banned and most of Cambodia's artists and intellectuals were killed. By the time Pol Pot was driven out by neighboring Vietnam in 1979, approximately two million Cambodians had died from execution, starvation, disease, and hard labor. In the following years of Vietnamese occupation and the Khmer Rouge's continuing guerrilla war, hundreds of thousands of Cambodians fled the country and became refugees.

In 1994, as peace was slowly restored to Cambodia, nine of these refugees returned and decided to revive the arts—not typically the first thing a devastated country focuses on after a war. But the young men had discovered the healing power of the arts while taking drawing classes when in a refugee camp and believed it could help children overcome the trauma of war. They founded Phare Ponleu Selpak (PPSA), or "the Brightness of the Arts," first offering drawing classes and then adding visual arts, music, theater, dance, circus arts, and even regular schooling.

Then, in 2013, the organization revived a long tradition by founding Phare, the Cambodian Circus. Phare shares the country's stories through performances that involve circus arts, theater, dance, and live music. Profits from the shows, which star PPSA graduates, fund the organization's free education programs.

With the circus back in town—and thriving—PPSA has helped rebuild the arts movement Pol Pot tried to wipe out, while providing children with life skills and helping the nation rediscover and reconnect with its cultural identity.

What if rocket launchers fired Ping-Pong balls instead of ballistic missiles?

A Chinese Ping-Pong player's show of good sportsmanship led two rival countries down the road to reconciliation. Welcome to "Ping-Pong diplomacy."

The Chinese and American Ping-Pong teams were in Nagoya, Japan, for the 1971 World Table Tennis Championships. China and the United States had been on bad terms for two decades, but both countries wanted to fix that.

Still, the Chinese players had been instructed not to socialize with their American rivals. So when Glenn Cowan unexpectedly boarded the Chinese team's bus, he was met with surprise and total silence. Minutes later, though, world champion Zhuang Zedong offered Cowan a gift: a silk screen of the Huangshan Mountains. Whether Zedong's gesture was as spontaneous as it appeared or set up by the Chinese government (as some have speculated over the years), it changed history.

The next day, Cowan gave Zedong a T-shirt with a peace sign and The Beatles' song title "Let It Be." China's leader, Chairman Mao Zedong (no relation to Zhuang), then invited the US team to China—the first official invitation to Americans since the Chinese Communist Party came to power in 1949. For eight days, the Americans toured the country and played friendly matches with their Chinese counterparts.

Relations between the two countries warmed. The Chinese team visited the United States. US president Richard Nixon made it easier to do business with and travel to and from China. He himself would visit—a first for a sitting president—and called his trip "the week that changed the world." All because of Ping-Pong.

What if the realities of war were only virtual realities?

Forget about car chases and shoot-'em-ups. Some video games turn play into an opportunity to build understanding by dropping players into a virtual version of a real-life conflict zone.

In the award-winning game *1979 Revolution: Black Friday*, you control the character Reza Shirazi, a photojournalist who becomes caught up in Iran's violent uprising against the shah, the king who has ruled his country since the 1940s. You try to remain neutral, but every choice has a consequence, from the seemingly minor to the definitely fatal.

The game is based on historical events and real stories from those who were there—freedom fighters, witnesses, and prisoners. The game's creator, Navid Khonsari, was himself raised in Tehran, Iran, until he was ten. His family moved to Canada after the Iranian Revolution, when the shah was overthrown and the country became an Islamic republic ruled by a supreme leader with ultimate political and religious authority.

Iranian authorities called *1979 Revolution* "anti-Iranian" and banned it. Khonsari was even accused of being a spy for the United States, where he now lives.

This hasn't stopped him. More recently, he's created the virtual-reality game *Blindfold*, which brings players back to Iran and its infamous Evin Prison, as well as *Hero*, a virtual-reality installation that takes participants to a bombing in Syria. Through these kinds of immersive storytelling, players face moral dilemmas and life-and-death situations, and get a sense of what it means to be surrounded by instability and violence.

Building understanding involves evoking empathy, emotion, and connection, Khonsari told an audience at the 2016 Games for Change Festival. That's what he and his company, iNK Stories, try to do, all the while creating entertaining and engaging experiences.

And if experiences in the virtual world can help keep history in the real world from repeating itself, all the better.

What if the balance of power was weighed on a teeter-totter?

Adults often think they know best, but it was children who led a war-torn South American country to peace.

By 1996, Colombia's civil war had been raging for over thirty years. Tens of thousands had been kidnapped or killed. Millions had fled their homes. And there was no end in sight.

"How can we learn to be peaceful if we don't understand what it means?" said then fifteen-year-old Farlis Calle, a teen activist from Apartadó, one of the country's most violent cities.

She and twenty-six other young Colombian leaders who had grown up with war and violence all their lives were invited to a workshop to talk about how to make Colombian children's lives better. The group then formed the Children's Movement for Peace. Their first action was to organize an election for Colombian children to vote on which rights were most important to them. Members of the movement received death threats,

but they pushed on. "They can kill some of us, but they can't kill us all," said Mayerly Sanchez, who was twelve years old when she joined the movement.

On October 25, 1996, nearly three million children went to the polls and voted for the right to life and the right to peace. Inspired by and newly aware of the war's impact on their children, ten million adults voted a year later on a Citizen's Mandate: to support the children's vote, to build peace, and to demand an end to child soldier recruitment and other atrocities of war. This mandate guided the presidential elections in 1998, with peace a key issue.

Although a peace agreement would come only in 2016, the Children's Movement for Peace—nominated several times for the Nobel Peace Prize—had got the talks started, proving that children know how to use their weight in the balancing act between war and peace.

What if an air strike was a cry for peace carried by the wind?

Your voice is basically vibrating air. And yet, as one refugee from the Democratic Republic of Congo discovered, it can be the most powerful weapon you have.

After war broke out in 1998, rebel soldiers stormed Baruani Ndume's village. They forced the people into their homes and then set the houses on fire. Ndume was young and small enough to squeeze out through a hole, and his mother told him to run. It was the last time he would see her.

After reaching a refugee camp in neighboring Tanzania, Ndume found life there was also very hard: too many people, too much violence, too little hope.

At the camp's school, though, Ndume learned about children's rights and how adults must accept those rights. In his teens, he started a radio program called *Sisi Kwa Sisi* (meaning "children for children"), during which he and other young people reported on the issues facing child refugees. He also used the show to let young listeners know about their rights. And because the program was broadcast in four countries (the Democratic Republic of Congo, Burundi, Rwanda, and Tanzania) and had thousands of listeners each week, he helped reunite many children who were separated from their families by the war.

In 2009, when he was sixteen years old, Ndume was awarded the International Children's Peace Prize. "It's my greatest wish," he told a film crew for KidsRights, an international children's rights organization, "that through radio, children all over the world will raise their voices and speak up so that their rights will be respected everywhere."

What if hand-to-hand combat happened only in boxing rings?

Muhammad Ali was the heavyweight boxing champion of the world, but his biggest fight was against the United States government.

In 1967, twenty-five-year-old Ali refused to be drafted into the Vietnam War. He opposed the war and believed he had no reason to fight the Vietcong. He had applied for exemptions as a conscientious objector and as a Muslim minister, but both were denied. So on the day he was to take the oath to join the army, he refused to step forward when his name was called.

Ali was arrested, convicted, stripped of his heavyweight title, and also had his boxing license suspended. He appealed his conviction and used his time to visit college campuses and speak out against the war. "Boxing is nothing like going to war with machine guns, bazookas, hand grenades, bomber airplanes," he said. "My intention is to box, to win a clean fight. But in war, the intention is to kill, kill, kill, kill, and continue killing innocent people."

As the new decade approached, the Vietnam War became increasingly unpopular with Americans. In 1970, Ali was allowed back in the ring, and the next year, the Supreme Court overturned his conviction. A free man, Ali did what he did best—"float like a butterfly, sting like a bee"—and went on to win the world heavyweight title two more times.

In 2005, more than thirty years after the US pulled out of Vietnam, Ali received the Presidential Medal of Freedom from the same country that had once condemned him. For Ali, taking a stand wasn't about approval but moral conviction: "A man who is not courageous enough to take risks will never accomplish anything in life."

What if words of war became a war of words?

Imagine going to a dinner party and ending up as part of a justice league of writers, battling censorship, imprisonment, and execution.

In 1921, British poet and playwright Catharine Amy Dawson-Scott created a dinner club she called PEN (an acronym for "poets, essayists, novelists" that was later expanded to include playwrights and editors) so writers could gather to enjoy one another's company. It was such a popular idea that PEN centers soon opened across Europe and then around the world, giving local and traveling writers a place to connect.

At first, talking politics at PEN was forbidden. But by the mid-1930s, Nazism was on the rise in Germany and PEN members realized they couldn't ignore the obvious: Books were being burned. Truths were being hidden. Writers were being silenced.

PEN began campaigning to help writers who were forced to leave their home countries, thrown in jail, and sometimes even sentenced to death because of what they wrote and the opinions they expressed. After the Second World War, the United Nations formally recognized PEN, allowing it to work with the international organization to provide even more support to writers around the world who want to write without risking jail time or their lives. And today its work is as important as ever: 90 percent of journalists' murders go unsolved, according to the World Association of Newspapers and News Publishers.

With centers in over one hundred countries, PEN International investigates the persecution and imprisonment of writers, journalists, bloggers, translators, and other publishing people, and works to help them regain their freedom. Its Writers in Prison Committee alone keeps track of seven hundred to nine hundred cases every year.

In an age of fake news, censorship, and propaganda, PEN International is fighting for truth, justice, and the writerly way.

What if we just asked more questions?

"To raise new questions, new possibilities, to regard old problems from a new angle, requires creative imagination," Albert Einstein once wrote. Because imagination has no limits, it's incredibly powerful: we can dream up the improbable and shape it into something new and exciting and truly possible.

When we ask questions starting with "What if … ?" we dare ourselves to think big and to think differently. And if we're brave enough, we can imagine something beyond the obvious and come up with what may at first seem like a truly wild idea.

Equally important is to start moving those wild ideas into the realm of possibilities … with critical thinking. At its core, critical thinking means carefully and objectively considering a problem or situation using what you already know and what you learn by asking relevant questions. It allows you to fill in the blanks, analyze information, discover other perspectives, evaluate strengths and weaknesses, and figure out who might be able to help. Every question asked—who, what, where, when, why, and how— potentially leads to another, making it easier for you to see the situation's bigger picture and come up with possible solutions.

The world may sometimes feel like it's in constant conflict, and our own lives may seem like one challenge after another. But it's impossible to solve problems, big or small, if you don't try. As you've read, even seemingly hopeless situations were improved when people imagined novel ways to make a positive impact on their community, their country, our world. By thinking big, they reunited families, saved lives, and even stopped a war.

What if *you* could change the world?

GLOSSARY

Balance of power: A situation where different countries or sides have about the same amount of power so one cannot dominate the other.

Ballistic missile: A weapon that is briefly guided in early flight, then relies on gravity and air resistance on its downward trajectory before detonating.

Basque: An inhabitant of a region in northern Spain and southern France. The Basques have their own language, history, and culture.

Civil war: An armed conflict between groups within the same country.

Conscientious objector: A person who refuses to join the military or carry a weapon on religious or moral grounds.

Draft: The selection of people for required military service.

Guerilla: A member of an independent, unofficial army that engages in irregular warfare, such as sabotage and raids, usually against official armed forces.

Incendiary bomb: An explosive device for the purpose of starting fires.

Islamic law: A set of moral and religious principles guiding the daily lives of Muslims.

Islamic State: A militant group that seized parts of Syria and Iraq and created its own state, known as a caliphate, governed by a strict interpretation of Islamic law.

Khmer Rouge: A Communist movement that took power in Cambodia in 1975.

Navy SEAL: An elite American special operations force trained for unconventional warfare. SEAL stands for Sea, Air, and Land.

Political party: A group of people who share ideas about how a country should be run and work together to get their candidates elected to government.

Refugee camp: A temporary place to live for people (called refugees) who have escaped or been forced from their own homes because of war or other dangers.

Theater of war: Any area—land, water, or air—where armed conflict takes place.

Vietcong: The Communist guerrilla soldiers who fought against the South Vietnamese government as well as its ally, the United States, during the Vietnam War.

ENDNOTES

p. 4: "We … imagine better." J.K. Rowling, quoted in J.K. Rowling, "The Fringe Benefits of Failure, and the Importance of Imagination," *Harvard Gazette*, June 5, 2008. Online.

p. 11: "We proved today … all the weapons." Didier Drogba, quoted in "Didier Drogba: Speech to Stop Civil War," uploaded by Arturo Rebolledo, June 21, 2016, on YouTube. Translated by the author.

p. 11: "I have won … peace in my country." Didier Drogba, quoted in Alex Hayes, "Didier Drogba Brings Peace to the Ivory Coast," *Telegraph*, August 8, 2007. Online.

p. 13: "You know … to enjoy ourselves." Letter from Bosnian refugees, quoted on the website of Clowns Without Borders International. Online.

p. 21: "Our responsibility … something about it." Thiat, quoted in *Rebel Music*, "Senegal: Ready for Change," aired May 28, 2015, on MTV.

p. 29: "How can we learn … what it means?" Farlis Calle, quoted in Sara Cameron, *Out of War: True Stories from the Frontlines of the Children's Movement for Peace in Colombia* (New York: Scholastic Press, 2001).

p. 29: "They … can't kill us all," Mayerly Sanchez, quoted on the website of the World's Children's Prize. Online.

p. 31: "It's my greatest wish … respected everywhere." Baruani Ndume, quoted on the website of KidsRights. Online.

p. 33: "Boxing is nothing like … killing innocent people." Muhammad Ali, quoted in NBC News: "Muhammad Ali on Not Going to War." NBC News video clip, January 17, 2012. Online.

p. 33: "A man … anything in life." Muhammad Ali, quoted in Tim Dahlberg, "Muhammad Ali Was a Man Who 'Stood for the World.'" *Globe and Mail*, June 4, 2016. Online.

p. 37: "To raise … creative imagination." Albert Einstein, quoted in Albert Einstein and Leopold Infeld, *The Evolution of Physics: The Growth of Ideas from Early Concepts to Relativity and Quanta* (Cambridge: Cambridge University Press, 1971).

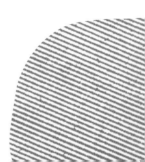

SELECTED SOURCES

PAGES 6 AND 7:

Desmond Doss Council. Desmond Doss: The Conscientious Objector. Online.

Herndon, Booton. *Redemption at Hacksaw Ridge: The Gripping True Story That Inspired the Movie*. Coldwater, MI: Remnant Publications, 2016.

PAGES 8 AND 9:

Food Not Bombs. Online.

Stockholm International Peace Research Institute. "Global Military Spending Remains High at $1.7 Trillion." Posted May 2, 2018. Online.

World Food Programme. "World Hunger Again on the Rise, Driven by Conflict and Climate Change, New UN Report Says." Posted September 15, 2017. Online.

PAGES 10 AND 11:

Lapinski, Jessica. *Raconte-moi: Didier Drogba*. Montreal: Petit Homme, 2016.

Wahl, Grant. "Soccer Savior." *Sports Illustrated*, May 24, 2010. Online.

PAGES 12 AND 13:

Clowns Without Borders International. Online.

Hassard, Jack. "The Ecology of Innovation in Teaching and Learning." National Education Policy Center. Posted May 24, 2013. Online.

PAGES 14 AND 15:

Diehl, Jörg. "Practicing Blitzkrieg in Basque Country: Hitler's Destruction of Guernica." *Der Spiegel*, April 26, 2007. Online.

Museo Nacional Centro de Arte Reina Sofía. Online.

Treasures of the World. "Guernica: Testimony of War." Produced by Barry Stoner. Aired 1999 on PBS. Online.

PAGES 16 AND 17:

Dance for Peace. "Ahmad Joudeh: Dance or Die." Online.

Elbaum, Rachel. "What Is ISIS? What You Need to Know About Islamic State in Iraq and Syria." NBC News, April 18, 2018. Online.

PAGE 18 AND 19:

Blake, John. "Two Enemies Discover a 'Higher Call' in Battle." CNN.com, March 9, 2013. Online.

Makos, Adam, with Larry Alexander. *A Higher Call*. New York: Berkley Caliber, 2012.

PAGES 20 AND 21:

Howden, Daniel. "Rap Revolution: Voices of Dissent in Senegal." *Independent*, February 20, 2012. Online.

Incorruptible. Directed by Elizabeth Chai Vasarhelyi. Charlevoix Entertainment, Little Monster Films, 2015.

Rebel Music. "Senegal: Ready for Change." Produced by Nusrat Durrani. Aired May 28, 2015, on MTV. Online.

PAGE 22 AND 23:

Phare Ponleu Selpak. "Phare: The Cambodian Circus." Online.

"Pol Pot." History.com, November 9, 2009. Online.

PAGES 24 AND 25:

Andrews, Evan. "How Ping-Pong Diplomacy Thawed the Cold War." History.com, October 19, 2018. Online.

Griffin, Nicholas. *Ping-Pong Diplomacy: The Secret History Behind the Game That Changed the World*. New York: Scribner, 2014.

PAGES 26 AND 27:

iNK Stories. Online.

"Khamenei Will Be Iran's Last Supreme Leader." *Newsweek*, November 17, 2009. Online.

Khonsari, Navid. "Empathy Overload: Choice Matters." Lecture presented at the 13th Annual Games for Change Festival, New York City, NY, June 24, 2016. Online.

Muncy, Julie. "*1979 Revolution: Black Friday*: Gripping Adventure Game Puts You in the Iranian Revolution." *Wired*, June 17, 2016. Online.

PAGES 28 AND 29:

Cameron, Sara. *Out of War: True Stories from the Frontlines of the Children's Movement for Peace in Colombia*. New York: Scholastic Press, 2001.

Pearl, Mariane. "Global Diary: A Child of War, Building Peace." *Glamour*, June 1, 2007. Online.

PAGES 30 AND 31:

Ikink, Inge. *Changemakers: The 10 International Children's Peace Prize Winners Tell Their Remarkable Stories*. Deventer, Netherlands: KidsRights, 2014. Online.

KidsRights. "Baruani Ndume." Online.

PAGES 32 AND 33:

Calamur, Krishnadev. "Muhammad Ali and Vietnam." *Atlantic*, June 4, 2016. Online.

Lipsyte, Robert. "Clay Refuses Army Oath; Stripped of Boxing Crown." *New York Times*, April 29, 1967. Online.

PAGES 34 AND 35:

Heslop, Andrew. "A New Level of Audacity for Impunity and Journalist Murders." World Association of Newspapers and News Publishers. Posted October 26, 2018. Online.

PEN International. Online.

PAGES 36 AND 37:

"Our Concept and Definition of Critical Thinking." Foundation for Critical Thinking, n.d. Online.

Watanabe-Crockett, Lee. "The Critical Thinking Skills Cheatsheet [Infographic]." Global Digital Citizen Foundation. Posted December 12, 2016. Online.

Owlkids Books acknowledges the financial support of the Canada Council for the Arts, the Ontario Arts Council, the Government of Canada through the Canada Book Fund (CBF), and the Government of Ontario through the Ontario Creates Book Initiative for our publishing activities.

Published in Canada by
Owlkids Books Inc.
1 Eglinton Avenue East
Toronto, ON M4P 3A1

Published in the United States by
Owlkids Books Inc.
1700 Fourth Street
Berkeley, CA 94710

Library of Congress Control Number: 2019947215

Library and Archives Canada Cataloguing in Publication

Title: What if soldiers fought with pillows? : true stories of imagination and courage / written by
   Heather Camlot ; illustrated by Serge Bloch.
Names: Camlot, Heather, author. | Bloch, Serge, illustrator.
Description: Includes bibliographical references.
Identifiers: Canadiana 20190134526 | ISBN 9781771473620 (hardcover)
Subjects: LCSH: Social action—History—Miscellanea—Juvenile literature.
| LCSH: Political
   participation—History—Miscellanea—Juvenile literature. | LCSH:
Children's questions and answers.
Classification: LCC HN13 .C36 2020 | DDC j303.48/4—dc23

Edited by Stacey Roderick
Designed by Alisa Baldwin

Manufactured in Guangzhou, Dongguan, China, in October 2019,
by Toppan Leefung Packaging & Printing (Dongguan) Co., Ltd.
Job #BAYDC67

A   B   C   D   E   F

ONTARIO ARTS COUNCIL
CONSEIL DES ARTS DE L'ONTARIO
an Ontario government agency
un organisme du gouvernement de l'Ontario

Canada Council   Conseil des Arts
for the Arts   du Canada

Canadä

Publisher of Chirp, Chickadee and OWL
www.owlkidsbooks.com

Owlkids Books is a division of bayard canada

ACKNOWLEDGMENTS

"*What if* Heather could find examples …?" Owlkids editorial director Karen Li wrote in an email, and in doing so transformed the original picture book idea for *What if …?* into the middle-grade nonfiction book you hold in your hands. What if, indeed! Thank you to Karen Li for seeing the bigger picture, to publisher Karen Boersma for inviting me into the Owlkids family, and to CANSCAIP for the introductions and continued support. I am indebted to Stacey Roderick for her editorial eye, spot-on suggestions, and ever-enthusiastic attitude. I am grateful to Anne Laurel Carter and the writers in her picturebook workshop for their encouragement and suggestions. Big thanks to my husband, Marc, for cheering me on; to my daughter, Juliana, for her critique; and to my son, Alex, who gave me the idea for this book one sleepless night, as well for its first profile, soccer legend (and former Montreal Impact player!) Didier Drogba.